# KILLER CREATURES

## Claire Llewellyn

KINGFISHER

NEW YORK

**KINGFISHER**
LONDON & NEW YORK

Copyright © 2008 by Kingfisher
Published in the United States by Kingfisher,
175 Fifth Ave., New York, NY 10010
Kingfisher is an imprint of Macmillan Children's Books, London.
All rights reserved.

Consultant: David Burnie

Illustrations by Steve Weston (represented by Linden Artists)
with additional artwork by Peter Bull Studio and Lee Gibbons

First published in 2008 by Kingfisher
First published in paperback in 2011 by Kingfisher

Distributed in the U.S. by Macmillan, 175 Fifth Ave., New York, NY 10010
Distributed in Canada by H.B. Fenn and Company Ltd., 34 Nixon Road, Bolton, Ontario L7E 1W2

LIBRARY OF CONGRESS CATALOGING-IN-PUBLICATION DATA
Llewellyn, Claire.
Navigators : killer creatures / Claire Llewellyn.—1st American ed.
p. cm.
Includes index.
ISBN 978-0-7534-6227-0
1. Predatory animals—Juvenile literature. 2. Dangerous animals—Juvenile
literature. I. Title. II. Title: Killer creatures.
QL758.L58 2008
591.6'5—dc22

2007047439

ISBN: 978-0-7534-6484-7

Kingfisher books are available for special promotions and premiums. For details contact:
Special Markets Department, Macmillan, 175 Fifth Ave., New York, NY 10010.

For more information, please visit www.kingfisherbooks.com

Printed in China
1 3 5 7 9 8 6 4 2
1TR/1010/WKT/SC(UG)/140MA

**Note to readers:** The website addresses listed in this book are correct at the time of publishing.
However, due to the ever-changing nature of the Internet, website addresses and content can change.
Websites can contain links that are unsuitable for children. The publisher cannot be held responsible
for changes in website addresses or content or for information obtained through third-party websites.
We strongly advise that Internet searches are supervised by an adult.

The publisher would like to thank the following for permission to reproduce their images. Every care has been taken to trace copyright holders.
However, if there have been unintentional omissions or failure to trace copyright holders, we apologize and will, if informed, endeavor to make
corrections in any future edition. (t = top, b = bottom, c = center, r = right, l = left)

Front cover Getty/Taxi; Back cover Nature Picture Library/Andy Rouse; Page 4lc Getty/Gallo/Heinrich van den Bergh; 4–5 Seapics/Kike Calvo; 5tl Natural History
Picture Agency (NHPA)/Rich Kirchner; 5tr Frank Lane Picture Agency (FLPA)/Minden Pictures; 5rc Corbis/Reuters; 5br Photolibrary/Frank Schneidermeyer; 6lc NHPA;
6–7 FLPA/Minden/Martin Harvey; 7t Getty/Gallo/Heinrich van den Bergh; 7c NHPA/Daryl Balfour; 7bl Nature PL/Martin Dohrn; 7br Getty/Steve Bloom; 8c FLPA/Minden
Pictures; 8b Nature PL/David Welling; 8br Corbis/Jeff Vanuga; 9tl Getty/NGS; 9tr Corbis/Jeff Vanuga; 9bl NHPA/Rich Kirchner; 9br Nature PL/Larry Michael; 10tr Science
Photo Library (SPL)/Andrew Syred; 10bl Seapics/Innerspace Visions; 11tc Corbis/Arthur Morris; 11c Corbis/ Terry W. Eggers; 11t Photolibrary/Daniel Cox; 11b Alamy/Steven
Kazlowski; 12tl Nature PL/Tony Heald; 12r Photolibrary/Richard Packwood; 13t Nature PL/Christophe Courteau; 13c Nature PL/Ingo Arndt; 13br Ardea/Jean-Paul Ferrero;
14tr Photolibrary/Tony Allen; 14bl Ardea/Mike Watson; 15t Corbis/Gerolf Kalt; 16tr Seapics; 16bl FLPA/Minden Pictures; 20c Corbis/Gary Bell; 20–21 Oceanwide
Images/Gary Bell; 20bl Nature PL/Jeff Rotman; 21tc FLPA/Panda Photo; 21b FLPA; 22br Seapics; 23 Getty/Digital Vision; 23cr Photolibrary/Frank Schneidermeyer;
23c Getty/Visuals Unlimited/Joe McDonald; 24tl Alamy; 24tr Nature PL/Daniel Gomez; 24bl PA/AP; 24–25 c and l SPL/Paul Whitten; 26 Photolibrary/Kathie Atkinson;
27tr FLPA/Minden Pictures; 27cr FLPA/Minden Pictures; 27b FLPA/Minden Pictures; 28tl Getty; 28tl FLPA/Minden Pictures; 28tr FLPA/Minden Pictures; 28br FLPA;
29cr Corbis/Wolfgang Kaehler; 29b NHPA/Daniel Heuclin; 30tr Nature PL/Anup Shah; 30 FLPA/Fritz Polking; 32cl Photolibrary/Juniors Bildarchiv; 32br Photolibrary/John
Downer; 33bl FLPA/Minden Pictures; 34cr FLPA/Minden Pictures; 34–35 Nature PL/Daniel Heuclin; 35cr SPL/David T. Roberts; 35b Corbis/Mark Baker; 36c FLPA/Minden
Pictures; 37 Animals/Animals/Roger de la Harpe; 36–37 Photolibrary/Joaquin Gutierrez Acha; 38tr Corbis/Robert Patrick; 38cl Photolibrary/OSF; 38b SPL/Eye of Science;
39tr SPL/David Scharf; 40tr Nature PL/Martin Dohrn; 40c Nature PL/Martin Dohrn; 41tl FLPA/Minden Pictures; 41tc FLPA/Minden Pictures; 42tr SPL/Roger Harris;
48tl Corbis/Ferdaus Shamim; 48tr Alamy/Adrian Sharratt; 48cr Nature PL/John Downer

# CONTENTS

# KILL OR BE KILLED

In the struggle to survive, many animals have become killer creatures, attacking to defend themselves or to satisfy their hunger. Some are solitary hunters, while others hunt in packs or even armies. Few corners of the planet—in the air, in water, or on land—are safe from predators.

## Sharks

A great white shark lives up to its nickname, "Jaws," as it grabs a mouthful of tuna. The great white is the ultimate ocean predator. Like other killer sharks, it relies on its sharp senses, speed, and terrifying power to locate and overwhelm seals and other prey.

- Location: Almost all oceans
- Habitat: Coastal waters
- Length: 20 ft. (6m)

## Big cats

A bloodied Bengal tiger reveals its fearsome fangs. Tigers, lions, and other big cats use stealth, speed, and sheer power to bring down prey such as deer.

- Location: Southern Asia
- Habitat: Rainforests, forests, and grasslands
- Length: 10 ft. (3m)

## Raptors

A harpy eagle flies off with a howler monkey in its grasp. Eagles, hawks, and falcons are the killers of the bird world. Known as raptors, they use their talons to stab prey and their beaks to rip apart flesh.

- Location: North and South America
- Habitat: Lowland rainforests
- Wingspan: 6.5 ft. (2m)

> A harpy eagle is armed with supersharp talons that are up to 5 in. (13cm) long—almost as long as a grizzly bear's claws.

## Wolves

A gray wolf tears into a kill. Like African wild dogs and hyenas, wolves hunt in packs, using teamwork, stamina, and speed to track their prey.

- Location: North America and Eurasia
- Habitat: Mountains, forests, and tundra
- Length: 5 ft. (1.5m)

## Amphibians

The brightly colored skin of the golden poison-arrow frog warns of toxins that can kill in seconds. The poison is a defense against predators.

- Location: Colombia, South America
- Habitat: Rainforests
- Length: 2 in. (5cm)

## Spiders

A Sydney funnel-web spider prepares to strike. Efficient killers, spiders inject venom through their fangs in order to paralyze or kill prey.

- Location: Eastern Australia
- Habitat: Forested uplands
- Body length: Almost 1.5 in. (3.5cm)

## Snakes

As a gaboon viper bites into a mouse, venom pumps out of its fangs. Not all snakes use venom to kill. Constrictors coil their bodies around their victims, hugging them to death.

- Location: Sub-Saharan Africa
- Habitat: Rainforests and savannas
- Length: 5 ft. (1.5m)

BIG CAT—any large, meat-eating wild animal that is related to the domestic cat

# BIG CATS

Long claws, daggerlike teeth, and powerful, crushing jaws—big cats have plenty of weapons. Add their sharp senses, stealth, speed, and power and you have some of the animal world's top killers. Most big cats are lone hunters, stalking their prey slowly and silently and then sprinting forward to pounce and deliver the killer bite.

## Teamwork

The lion is the only big cat that lives and hunts in groups. Fleet-footed lionesses do most of the hunting. Step by step, they approach their prey—a herd of antelope, wildebeests, or zebras. Suddenly, one lioness breaks away to make a kill while the others lend support from the sides.

**A lioness closes in on a young kudu antelope.**

## Climbing cats

Leopards drag antelope and other prey up trees, out of the way of scavengers. Like all big cats, leopards use their fanglike canine teeth to grasp victims around the throat, choking them to death.

> If a lion cub is attacked and killed, its mother will eat the corpse.

## Killer jaws

Cats use their jagged carnassial teeth, which slice against one another like scissors, to cut up their kill. Small front teeth called incisors nibble flesh from the bones.

A feeding tiger defends its kill.

http://animal.discovery.com/guides/atoz/bcats.html

## Living in a pride

Hunting together allows lions to bring down larger prey, providing food for the whole pride. The males protect the kill from hungry scavengers, giving the cubs more time to eat their share.

"So have I heard on
Africa's burning shore,
A hungry lion give a grievous roar."

**William Barnes Rhodes (1772–1826)**
*from the opera* Bombastes Furioso, *1810*

## ⊜ DEADLY SPRINTER

A cheetah, the quickest animal on land, accelerates faster than most cars, reaching a top speed of almost 60 mph (95km/h) in 3–4 seconds. Unlike other big cats, a cheetah cannot retract, or pull back, its claws inside its paws. Instead, the claws work like the spikes on a track-and-field sprinter's shoes, helping the cheetah grip the ground. The life-or-death chase across the grassland is usually over in 20 seconds.

*lightweight body with long, thin, and muscular legs*

*Flexible spine powers huge bounds of up to 23 ft. (7m).*

## Night vision

Most cats hunt at night. At the back of their eyes is a golden layer, the tapetum, which shines when caught in light. It helps the eyes absorb extra light, boosting a cat's night vision.

# WOLVES OF THE TAIGA

**TAIGA**—a coniferous forest stretching across Asia, northern Europe, and North America

Wolves live and hunt in packs that contain up to 30 animals. As soon as a pack detects prey—such as herd of caribou or elk—it gives chase, honing in on any animal that lags behind. Sharp teeth snap at the victim's heels, slowing it down so that other pack members can get a grip on it. When prey is brought down, the wolves rip at its flesh. For large victims, such as elk, death is often slow.

## Feeding time

Wolf packs share their food, but there is a strict pecking order. First to feed are the pack leaders—the alpha male and female. Once they give a signal, the rest of the pack can join in. The wolves devour the kill, crushing bones to reach the rich, fatty marrow inside and leaving behind little waste.

**Wolves are intelligent animals and use calls and physical gestures to communicate with one another.**

*prey animal*

*Low head, low ears, low tail—this wolf is under pressure!*

*Eyes give sharp, binocular vision.*

*1-in. (2.5-cm)-long canine teeth grasp and rip prey.*

> A wolf needs an average of 3.3 lbs. (1.5kg) of meat per day. A large kill, such as a bison, will last a pack of wolves one week.

**Bear trouble**

Gray wolves in Alaska attempt to defend their kill from a hungry grizzly bear. Wolves and bears make uneasy neighbors. Bears are big and dangerous, but wolf packs can snatch and kill young bear cubs.

## ⊖ STAMINA AND SPEED

Wolves are muscular and, during a chase, can reach a top speed of 35 mph (56km/h). At other times, wolves prefer to trot, their long, strong legs covering around 3 ft. (1m) with each stride. They can keep up this pace for hours, covering 60 mi. (100km) in a single night.

*Each wolf runs in the footprints made by the pack's leader.*

*Large front feet prevent a wolf from sinking into soft snow.*

*Long hair makes a wolf look larger.*

"The aim of life was meat. Life itself was meat. Life lived on life. There were the eaters and the eaten. The law was: EAT OR BE EATEN."

**Jack London (1876–1916)**
*from the novel* **White Fang,** *1906*

*Sensitive ears can hear prey up to 10 mi. (16km) away.*

*A wolf's nose can detect prey up to 1 mi. (2km) away.*

**Pack discipline**

A strict social order in a pack prevents scuffles from escalating into fights. Young wolves give way to older animals and the weak submit to the strong. All pups develop strength and hunting skills through play fights like these.

www.defenders.org/wildlife_and_habitat/wildlife/wolf_gray.php

# ARCTIC GIANTS

ARCTIC OCEAN—the freezing ocean that surrounds the North Pole

The largest of all land carnivores, polar bears are also at home in the water, where their size, power, and swimming ability allow them to catch walrus and whales. More commonly, the bears hunt ringed seals near their breathing holes. When a bear senses an approaching seal, it punches the ice with its paw, grabs the seal's head in its jaws, and yanks the body up onto the ice.

cross section through hair, shown 350 times bigger than real size

"Something in the bear's presence made [Lyra] feel close to coldness, danger, brutal power . . ."

**Philip Pullman (born 1946)**
*from the novel* Northern Lights, *1995*

*Long outer hairs are hollow, trapping warm air close to the bear's body.*

## Bear legs

On thin ice, the polar bear's enormous feet help spread its weight over a large area. In water, the paws act like paddles. Polar bears swim with their front legs, stretching out their back legs to work like a rudder.

## Learning to hunt

After killing a seal, a polar bear rips open the carcass and, with her cub, feeds on the meat and blubber. Later the bears will roll in the snow to wash the blood from their coats. Females teach their cubs the art of stalking seals, but many attempts fail when the cubs fidget and give the bears away.

## Out at sea

Polar bears are supreme swimmers and have been seen 60 mi. (100km) from land, still powering through the water. In pursuit of prey, they can dive as deep as 15 ft. (4.5m) and can stay below the surface for more than one minute.

> A large male polar bear on its hind feet stands more than 10 ft. (3m) tall and weighs more than nine adult humans.

## Big brown bear

Grizzly bears are found in the frozen regions of Russia and North America. These formidable hunters kill prey as large as a moose but also catch fish and dig out burrowing creatures such as ground squirrels.

*Strong jaws and a variety of teeth allow grizzlies to feed on any type of food.*

*The grizzly's powerful front paws are equipped with claws that are up to 6 in. (15cm) long.*

*The beluga whale's tail thrashes wildly.*

*short, curved claws for grabbing prey*

*white beluga whale, a rare catch for a polar bear*

www.polarbearsinternational.org

## ⊖ NOSY NEIGHBOR

Polar bears are not usually man-eaters, but hungry ones can pose a dangerous threat to humans. A television camera operator once came face-to-face with a bear through the window of his cabin. He fired a flare gun to scare it off, but the bear came back—twice. On nights like that, it must be difficult to sleep!

*A polar bear's feet pads (and nose) are its only furless body parts.*

## CRUSHING JAWS

Hyenas have massive jaws that are filled with strong teeth. Their sharp canine teeth tear at a victim's skin, while the molars are so powerful that they can chew through a zebra's thighbone to reach the tasty marrow inside.

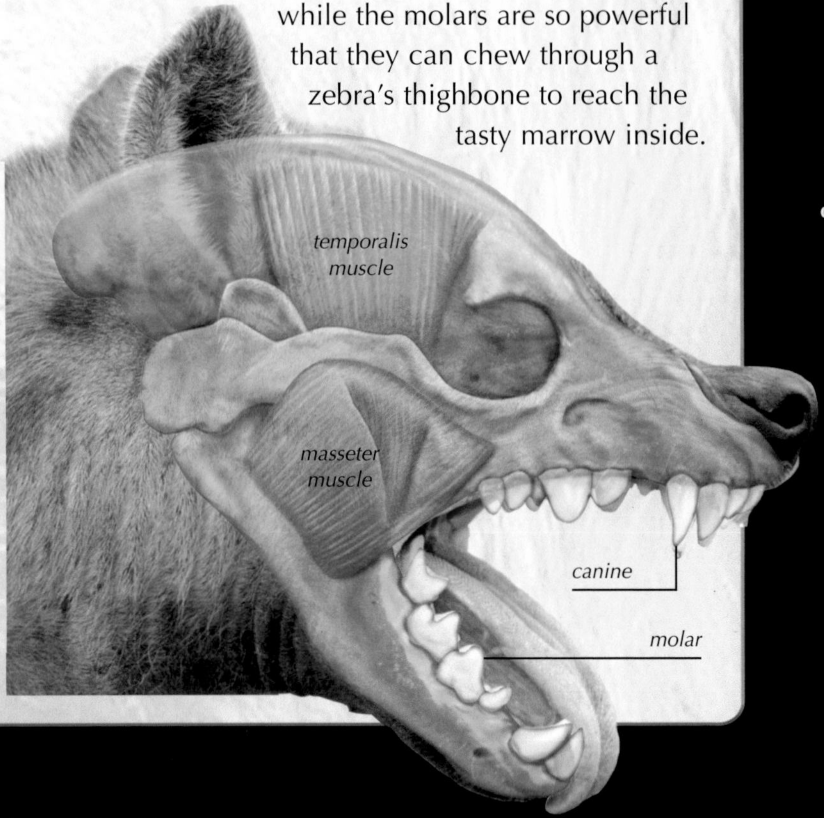

*temporalis muscle*

*masseter muscle*

*canine*

*molar*

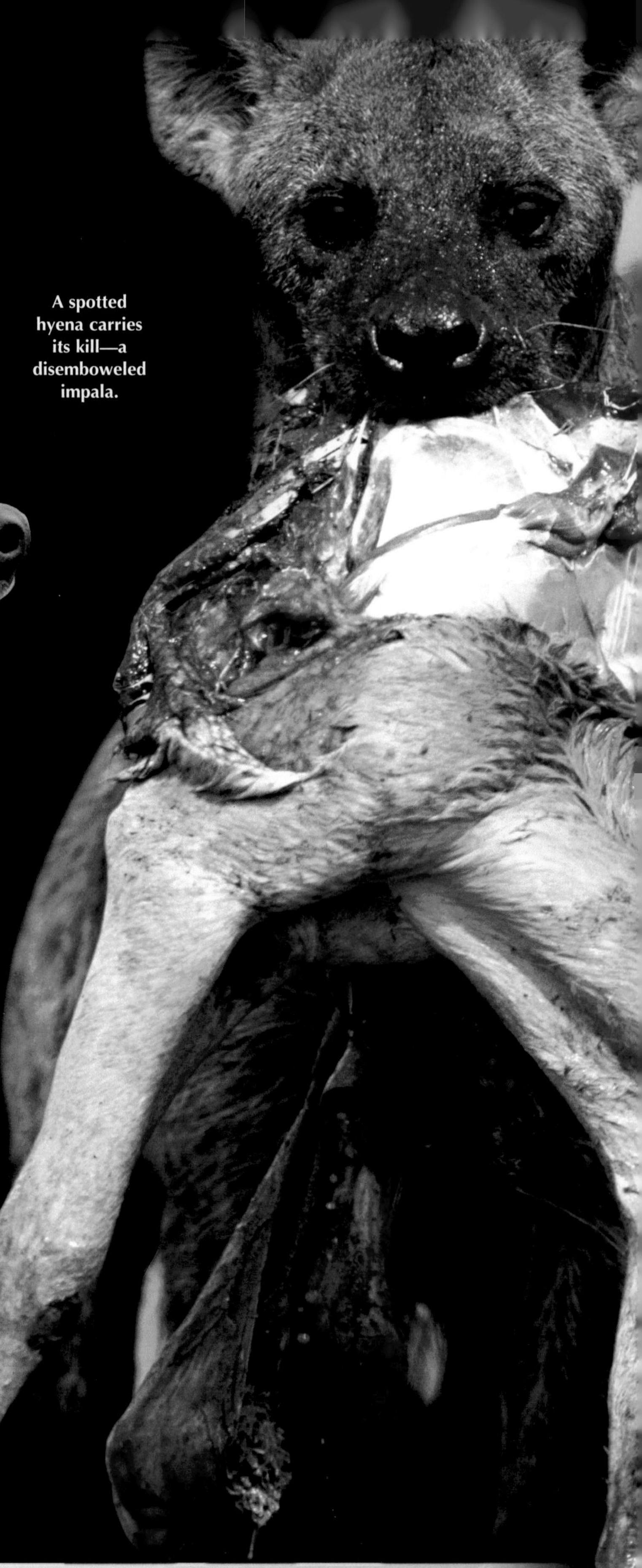

A spotted hyena carries its kill—a disemboweled impala.

# PACK HUNTERS

Hyenas hunt in packs, which helps them bring down large prey such as antelope and zebras. These fearless, fast, and lightly built hunters pursue their prey over long distances, taking turns leading the pack so that no individual gets too tired. Other pack hunters include Australian dingoes and African hunting dogs.

> Four out of every five attacks by African wild dogs ends in a successful kill.

*African
wild dog*

**A female spotted
hyena faces up to
a pair of snarling
African wild dogs.**

## Food fight
Both hyenas and wild dogs live on the
savanna grasslands of Africa. Packs
of hyenas will charge at wild dogs in an
attempt to steal their kill. Who wins will
depend on speed, aggression, and the
number of animals in each pack.

## Dog meat
Once an animal has been caught by
a pack of wild dogs, it is ripped apart.
The dogs hold down their kill before
hyenas, lions, and vultures move in
to pick at the remains.

# Night prowlers
The hyena looks like a dog but
belongs to a different animal family.
Hyenas are efficient scavengers and
skilled predators. They hunt at night
in small groups, killing much larger
prey. With strong jaws and powerful
digestive systems, they can eat and
extract nutrition even from their
victims' teeth and bones.

**Dingoes kill
kangaroos,
wallabies, and
smaller prey
such as this
monitor lizard.**

"Hyenas are larger and stronger,
but wild dogs attack in formation,
like a crack squad of commandos."

**Steve Leonard (born 1972)**
*British wildlife presenter and writer*

## Wild dog down under
Australian dingoes are descended from
wolflike dogs. They have been known
to attack children, so in dingo country
parents need to be aware of this danger.

# PREDATORY PIRANHAS

Piranhas are small freshwater fish that live in the rivers of South America. They have strong, upturned jaws like those of a bulldog and very sharp teeth. Not all species of piranhas are aggressive, but those that are have fearsome reputations. When piranhas are hungry and gang up in a school, they work together as one ferocious killing machine, targeting birds, rodents, frogs, and young caimans.

**Caught by a caiman**
A school of 20–30 piranhas may be a threat to a young caiman, but this lone fish stands no chance against a fully grown black caiman.

*An excited piranha turns on another. Even though these fish hunt together, within a school every fish is out for itself.*

## ● KILLER JAWS

A piranha's upper and lower teeth fit together so neatly that they can remove a perfect crescent-shaped chunk of flesh. Amazonian Indians have used the razor-sharp teeth for sharpening darts, shaving, and cutting.

**During the dry season, piranhas can be stranded in small lakes with little food. This makes them even more aggressive.**

*jaw packed with triangular teeth*

> In Brazil, around 1,200 cattle are killed by piranhas every year.

## Feeding frenzy

A young heron has fallen from its treetop nest into a river. Within seconds, its struggles have alerted a school of red-bellied piranhas. Smaller fish size up the prey, taking a few test bites before larger piranhas drag the bird below the surface.

www.extremescience.com/Piranha.htm

*Nostrils can detect a single drop of blood in 53 gal. (200L) of water.*

# SAVAGE SHARKS

VIBRATION—*a rippling movement through air or water*

If any animal has the reputation of killer creature, it is the shark. Sleek and efficient predators with tiptop senses and massive jaws, sharks hunt prey as large as elephant seals and squids. Some sharks circle their prey and disable it before the kill. Others attack by surprise from below.

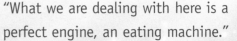

"What we are dealing with here is a perfect engine, an eating machine."

**Matt Hooper**
*fictional marine biologist in the movie Jaws, 1975*

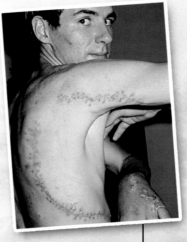

### Man-eater?

A survivor of a great white shark attack displays his stitches. Great whites are more feared than any other creature in the ocean—and with good reason. They carry out more attacks than any other type of shark.

### Shark senses

Sharks use many senses to find their prey. They detect vibrations (movements) and even faint trails of blood from wounded creatures. They also sense the weak electrical signals given off by all living things.

skin pore

*The ampullae of Lorenzini are sense organs on a shark's snout that detect electrical signals.*

sea lion

scalloped hammerhead shark

> In 2006, there were 62 unprovoked shark attacks on humans.

*Gills take in oxygen from the water.*

## TEETH

A shark's jaws are lined with rows of teeth. Some species have long, narrow, needlelike teeth for spearing fish and other small prey. Those that feed on larger animals have broad, serrated teeth to tear off chunks of flesh. Like disposable razor blades, shark teeth don't last long and are replaced as they break or wear out.

*serrated edge for cutting*

*muscular tail fin*

*gallbladder*

*stomach*

*streamlined body*

*A large liver helps a shark float.*

## Strength and speed

A great white smashes into its prey at around 30 mph (48km/h). In the split second before impact, it lifts its snout and leads with its upper jaws. The force of the attack carries the shark up out of the water with 220 lbs. (100kg) of meat in its mouth.

# FEROCIOUS ORCAS

ORCA—a large, predatory member of the dolphin family; also known as a killer whale

Orcas, also known as killer whales, are giants of the oceans. These mammals, which are a type of dolphin, can grow up to 30 ft. (9m) long and live in family groups called pods. Fast, fierce, and intelligent hunters, orcas work together to kill prey that is a lot bigger than themselves, such as great white sharks and humpback whales, as well as hundreds of smaller species.

## Athletes of the sea

Killer whales are remarkably agile for their size. They chase and catch fast-moving penguins and fish and even snap ducks out of the air. They toss their victims out of the water before swallowing them whole.

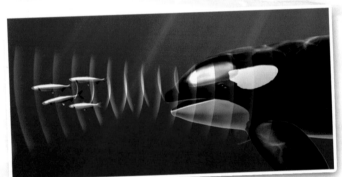

## Sound hunters

Killer whales use a hunting technique called echolocation, which is especially useful in deep, murky water. They send out a stream of high-pitched clicks and then listen for the echoes that bounce back off their prey.

*On the shore, sea lion pups are vulnerable and slow.*

> There is no documented instance of a wild orca killing a human being.

# Beach raider

A killer whale surfs onto a beach where sea lion pups are playing on the shore. It seizes a pup in its huge jaws and then flops back into the water to be washed out to sea. This is a tricky maneuver, but the reward of sea lion meat is worth the risk of getting stranded.

"If they'd wanted to, they could have tossed me and my kayak high into the air with just a flick of their tail."

**Steve Leonard (born 1972)**
*British wildlife presenter and writer*

*An orca zooms in for the kill at up to 37 mph (60km/h).*

**An orca hunts sea lion pups off the coast of Patagonia, Argentina.**

## ⊖ MASTER HUNTERS

Killer whales are inventive hunters. As well as using echolocation to find prey, they also make use of other techniques, including herding and trapping. They employ different methods for different types of prey.

*Orcas herd schools of herring into a tight ball and then slap them with their powerful tails to stun the fish.*

*After separating a whale calf from its mother, three orcas block off its route up to the surface to breathe.*

*While staking out a seal hidden in an underwater cave, these orcas hunt and breathe in a relay manner.*

*Orcas head butt ice floes to tip off penguins and seals or whip up the water with their tails to slide them off.*

# STINGERS OF THE SEA

In the warm, clear waters off northern Australia lies the Great Barrier Reef, the world's largest system of coral reefs. Built by the skeletons of tiny coral polyps, it stretches for more than 1,240 mi. (2,000km). The reef supports an astonishing variety of life, including more than 400 different corals. But divers beware! Lurking in these blue waters are some of the deadliest creatures in the sea.

> "In Australia, jellyfish season kicks off in November . . . Swarms of 3,500–4,000 jellyfish are not uncommon."
>
> **Steve Leonard (born 1972)**
> *British wildlife presenter and writer*

## Blue-ringed octopus

With a body the size of a golf ball, the blue-ringed octopus contains enough poison to kill ten people. The danger lies in the bite from its parrotlike beak, which is sharp enough to pierce a diver's wetsuit.

## ⬤ DEATH BY STINGRAY

Stingrays have venomous spines on the ends of their tails for protection. Steve Irwin, an Australian conservationist, was killed in 2006 when a stingray whipped its tail barb into his chest and damaged his heart.

**diver with southern stingray**

> The largest stingrays are 6 ft. (1.8m) wide and 14 ft. (4.2m) long, including their tails.

## Box jellyfish

The box jellyfish trails a mass of tentacles, packed with stinging cells called nematocysts. Swimmers are easily stung by this jellyfish. The pain is excruciating, and without antivenin, a victim can die in only four minutes.

**Made up of 95 percent water, the box jellyfish is almost invisible.**

*Microscopic, touch-sensitive hairs at the end of each spine trigger the release of poison.*

## Stonefish

The stonefish is the world's most poisonous fish. It lies quietly on coral, perfectly camouflaged. A slow mover, it needs a defense: 13 spines along its back that release a deadly poison when touched.

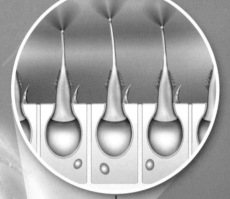

*Each tentacle carries millions of stinging cells called nematocysts. They have microscopic threads that explode on contact with prey.*

## Scary senses

A snake can sense vibrations through the ground, alerting it to nearby prey. It also picks up scents with its tongue. The tongue wipes airborne particles onto the roof of the mouth, where special cells send messages to the snake's brain, allowing it to identify the scent.

*The diamondback rattlesnake is named for its diamond-shaped markings.*

*The tail rattle makes sounds to warn off predators.*

# VENOMOUS SNAKES

With its slithering body and lightning speed, the snake is one of the most feared animal hunters. Many venomous snakes lie in wait for their prey. When a victim comes near, a snake rears up and strikes, injecting lethal venom from its fangs. Venom is an intelligent way of attacking dangerous prey with little physical contact. The poison paralyzes or kills quickly and may even begin to break down the body for digestion.

### Sea snakes

Found in tropical waters, sea snakes are among the most poisonous reptiles. Luckily, they rarely come into contact with humans and are not aggressive. One exception is the beaked sea snake of Australia. It carries out 90 percent of all fatal sea snake attacks.

> Australia is home to 11 of the top 12 most venomous land snakes.

## Spraying venom

As well as injecting prey, a cobra spits venom to defend itself. It can hit an enemy's eyes from as far away as 8 ft. (2.4m), causing temporary blindness.

*A snake detects smells with its nostrils, as well as with the cells of the Jacobson's organ in its mouth.*

*The forked tongue collects scent particles from the air as it flicks back and forth.*

"When you see a rattlesnake poised to strike you, do not wait until he has struck before you crush him."

**Franklin D. Roosevelt (1882–1945)**
*U.S. president, 1933–1945*

## ⊖ CAMOUFLAGED KILLERS

With no limbs, many snakes cannot chase prey. Instead, they wait for prey to come to them. They have such excellent camouflage that they are almost impossible to see, especially because they stay so still. Depending on their habitat, snakes have colors and markings that blend in with leaves, vines, sand, or rocks.

**A gaboon viper's markings resemble leaf litter.**

### Venom

Special glands produce venom, which is squeezed along tiny tubes and then into the hollow fangs. The venom is forced through small openings in the fangs and injected into puncture wounds made by the sharp fang tips.

*collared lizard*

www.rattlesnakes.com

# CONSTRICTOR CRUSH

Constrictors, such as boas, pythons, and anacondas, kill with power, not poison. When these snakes strike, they rapidly wrap muscular coils around their prey's body. Each time the victim breathes out, the coils tighten a little more so that it cannot breathe in. The tight squeeze also stops the prey's blood from flowing. Unable to pump blood, the heart comes to a fatal standstill.

## South American giant

The anaconda is the world's heaviest snake, weighing 440 lbs. (200kg) or more. It lives in or near water, catching capybaras and other animals that come to drink, as well as river turtles and caimans.

**young red-tail boa constricting a mouse**

## A mouse's fate

While suffocating its prey, a boa constrictor keeps a firm grip with sharp, hooked teeth. These teeth are not used for chewing, however, so the boa must swallow its victim whole.

## ● EXPLODING PYTHON

In Everglades National Park in Florida, the remains of an alligator were found sticking out of a dead Burmese python in 2005. The snake's stomach had been ripped open by the alligator's claws.

alligator's tail

burst stomach

python's tail

> The reticulated python is the world's longest snake. It can grow up to 30 ft. (9m) long.

*Backward-facing teeth drag in food.*

*breathing tube*

*jaws joined by flexible ligaments*

## Stretchy jaws

A snake's jaws are joined by ligaments that stretch to give it the necessary width to eat its supersize meals. The snake can breathe with its mouth full because it has a movable breathing tube located at the front of the lower jaw.

*A constrictor's ribs can move apart to make room for swallowed prey.*

"None of them knew the limits of [Kaa the python's] power, none of them could look him in the face, and none had ever come alive out of his hug."

**Rudyard Kipling (1865–1936)**
*from the novel* The Jungle Book, *1894*

## Down in one

A boa usually swallows prey headfirst so that the legs do not get stuck in its throat. The snake coats its dinner with slippery saliva and then uses strong muscles to push the food down into its stomach. There, powerful juices dissolve the flesh and bones.

http://animals.nationalgeographic.com/animals/reptiles/boa-constrictor.html

# DANGEROUS AMPHIBIANS

The world's most poisonous animal is a small amphibian from the rainforests of Colombia. To deter predators, the golden poison-arrow (or dart) frog has deadly toxins in its skin that attack the nervous system, rapidly causing heart failure. The cane toad is another amphibian that produces poisons in its skin for self-defense.

NERVOUS SYSTEM—*the brain, spinal cord, and nerves, which collect and respond to information about the state of the body*

## Poisonous toad

The cane toad, native to Central and South America, is very poisonous. Glands on its shoulders produce a milky poison that contains a deadly cocktail of 14 chemicals that cause convulsions and death. Introduced into Australia in the 1930s to control insect pests, the 4.4-lb. (2-kg) toad is now poisoning rare native species.

*reservoir of milky poison*

*Poison glands lie under the warty skin.*

*The rodent is devoured headfirst by the hungry toad, whose diet also includes insects and small reptiles.*

> Poison-arrow frogs get their name because the Chocó people of Central America rub the poison on the darts (arrows) they use to hunt.

www.poisondartfrog.co.uk

*An ant's body contains poisons— if a frog preys on the ant, the poisons transfer to the frog.*

## Deadly diet

A poison-arrow frog's poison comes from its diet of ants, termites, beetles, and centipedes. These creepy-crawlies absorb poisonous chemicals from the plants they eat. Frogs that are moved to a zoo lose their toxicity because they are not eating their natural diets.

**Cane toads hunt at night. They locate prey by noticing movements or by tracking their scents.**

## Color code

During the day, this poison-arrow frog is protected by its colors and pattern, which warn other animals that it is best left alone. At night, predators, such as this tarantula, are deterred by the taste of the frog's skin.

**green poison-arrow frog and tarantula**

**golden poison-arrow frog**

"Even crocodiles have been found dead with cane toads in their mouths."

**Mary Summerill (born 1958)**
*Presenter of the BBC documentary series Wild Down Under, 2003*

## ● HOW TOXIC ARE THEY?

A golden poison-arrow frog is only 2 in. (5cm) long, but its body contains enough poison to kill ten humans—or an astonishing 25,000 mice. How does that compare to other poisonous creatures?

**Golden poison-arrow frog could kill 25,000 mice.**

**Black widow could kill 700 mice.**

**King cobra could kill 3,500 mice.**

LIZARD—a type of reptile with four legs, a tail, and scaly skin

A Komodo uses its tongue to sniff for potential meals.

A Komodo's saliva contains more than 60 types of bacteria.

**A Komodo can weigh up to 440 lbs. (200kg)— more than two grown men.**

## Deadly saliva

Komodo dragons produce saliva that is full of harmful bacteria, which works like a primitive venom. If prey is wounded but manages to escape, it will die from the infected wound and the dragon will find and eat it.

# LETHAL LIZARDS

Most lizards are carnivorous, but two species have serious bites that can be dangerous to humans. One is the Gila (pronounced "hee-la") monster, which lives in deserts in Mexico and the southwestern United States. The other is a huge monitor lizard, the Komodo dragon, whose mouth is full of deadly bacteria. It is the world's largest lizard and lives on four islands in Indonesia.

## ⊖ FATAL ATTACK

Tragically, in 2007 a Komodo killed an eight-year-old boy. The animal mauled and bit the child, shaking him viciously from side to side. His family drove off the dragon, but the boy died from excessive bleeding.

thick, strong neck

scaly, leathery hide

powerful limbs

> The Komodo dragon can detect a potential meal from 3 mi. (5km) away, using its flicking tongue to sniff the air.

# Scary monster

The Gila monster is a slow-moving lizard. It tries to avoid confrontation if it can by hissing at any animals that challenge it. As a last resort, the Gila will bite, chewing to activate glands in its jaw that produce a poisonous saliva. The toxins, which flow in through the wound, cause paralysis. The Gila's eye-catching color and skin patterns warn enemies that it is poisonous.

### Dinner for six

Six Komodo dragons devour a goat. Komodos move swiftly for their size and attack water buffalo, boars, and deer. They pin down and rip apart prey with their massive claws. Unfussy diners, Komodos eat carrion, too.

*A Gila's beadlike, scaly skin is black with pink and yellow markings.*

**Baby rats are attacked by a Gila monster.**

"The breath is very fetid and its odor can be detected at some little distance."

**Scientific American magazine, 1890**

# KILLER CROCODILIANS

CROCODILIAN—a member of a group of reptiles that includes crocodiles, alligators, and gavials

They might look like prehistoric beasts, but crocodiles and alligators are alive today, lurking in rivers and lakes. These reptiles are found in subtropical and tropical parts of the world, where the sun warms their cold-blooded bodies and turns them into agile hunters. The saltwater crocodile can grow as long as 16 ft. (5m). It devours fish, other crocodiles, birds, mammals—and, sometimes, unlucky humans.

## Big snapper
The gavial nimbly catches fish by sweeping through the water with its long, narrow snout. Its needlelike teeth are perfect for spearing slippery prey.

## Deadly grip

A Nile crocodile clamps its jaws around a gazelle's neck in a Kenyan game park. Prey this large is a challenge for crocodiles because they cannot chew. They have to spin an animal until it breaks apart.

 > Crocodiles and alligators are believed to kill around 2,000 people every year.

*Nostrils are set high up on the skull so that the crocodile can breathe while hiding in the water.*

### New teeth for old

Crocodiles have around 60 teeth. They are designed for grabbing prey rather than cutting through flesh. To help break down large chunks of meat, crocodilians swallow stones. These churn around in one part of their stomachs, grinding up the food.

*Leathery skin is reinforced with bony, armored plates called scutes.*

"Don't think there are no crocodiles because the water is calm."

***Malaysian proverb***

## ⊖ SHOCK ATTACK

A crocodile's eyes, ears, and nostrils are on top of its head, allowing it to lie low in the water and still see, hear, smell, and breathe. To save energy, crocodiles wait, motionless, until a meal approaches . . .

*Resembling a log in the river, this Nile crocodile is unseen by its prey—a zebra on its way down to drink.*

*The crocodile explodes up out of the water in a lethal burst, clamping its jaws around the zebra's muzzle.*

*The terrified zebra slips on the muddy riverbank. Unable to struggle free, it is dragged into deeper water.*

*The crocodile spins the victim, drowning it or crushing its spine, and then breaks the body into chunks.*

*Red howler monkeys leap around and call frantically to one another in panic.*

*The canopy hides sloths, lizards, rodents, birds, and many other types of prey.*

## ⊖ SILENT HUNTER

Owls hunt at night. Their huge eyes help them see in low light, while their ears alert them to every rustle. The owl's fringed feathers muffle the sound of its wings, so prey rarely hears it coming.

**Tengmalm's owl with a mouse**

# RAPTOR RAID

Eagles, falcons, and other raptors have exceptional sight and hearing, plus the speed, strength, and lethal talons needed to catch and kill their prey. These birds use different forms of attack. A peregrine falcon drops like a stone to snatch a pigeon in midair. A golden eagle flies in low from the side to take its prey by surprise. The still-warm body is carried to a nearby perch and then ripped apart by the bird's powerful beak.

Bloody beak

A golden eagle uses its hooked beak to butcher a hare. Gripping the body with its sharp talons, it eats the meat and organs but discards the bones and fur. Owls swallow prey whole but later cough up a neat pellet of bones, feathers, and fur.

 > The peregrine falcon dives at speeds of almost 200 mph (320km/h), making it the fastest animal alive today.

*Startled scarlet macaws scatter noisily.*

*feathered crest raised during an attack*

## Death in the forest

A harpy eagle snatches a red howler monkey from the rainforest canopy, piercing the internal organs with its needle-sharp talons. This skillful hunter maneuvers itself easily through the dense trees and may travel as fast as 50 mph (80km/h) when it dives in on its prey.

www.sandiegozoo.org/animalbytes/t-harpy_eagle.html

## Curved claws
The talons of this harpy eagle chick will grow up to an amazing 5 in. (13cm) long.

## Black widow

This female black widow is eating her partner after mating with him. Despite their name and reputation, however, black widows do not always do this. The female is much more deadly to humans. With venom 15 times deadlier than a rattlesnake's, her bite can cause breathing problems and muscle cramps.

*Ultrasensitive hairs pick up sensations from the surrounding area.*

"A dark leg quivered in the milk-chocolate earth, then another, and another, until the whole tarantula was revealed."

**Nigel Marven (born 1960)**
*British wildlife presenter and writer*

# DEADLY ARACHNIDS

Spiders use venom to paralyze or kill their prey. The venom is made in a spider's poison glands and then squeezed along a tube until it shoots out through the spider's fangs. Different venoms work in different ways— some affect muscles and nerves, leading to cramps and paralysis, while others kill tissue surrounding the bite, resulting in scars that are slow to heal. Only around 100 species of spiders have venom that is harmful to people.

*The lifeless male, paralyzed by a bite, is wrapped up in silk.*

## Super sight

A jumping spider can spy prey from 12 in. (30cm) away, due to four pairs of eyes. The two largest eyes move independently, which is why they appear in different colors here.

ARACHNID—an animal such as a spider or scorpion

> The Goliath bird-eating spider of South America is the world's largest spider, with a leg span of 10 in. (26cm).

**A female black widow prepares to eat her mate.**

## ⊖ SECRET WEAPON

Bird-eating spiders, or tarantulas, can give painful bites. To attack, they raise the front of the body with legs high up in the air and then strike using their fangs like pickaxes. Some tarantulas release clouds of hairs from their legs. These hairs have microscopic barbs that stick to the skin— or eyes—and are very difficult to remove.

### On the boat from Brazil

Known for its speed and aggression, the Brazilian wandering spider is one of the world's deadliest spiders. It sometimes appears in Europe, hidden among bananas shipped from Central or South America.

*The underside of the female's rounded abdomen has a red, hourglass-shaped marking.*

*pedipalp— sensory feeler for tasting food*

### Dangerous Australian

The Sydney funnel-web spider wanders into houses in towns and cities. It bites with fangs that are strong enough to pierce a fingernail. Victims must find a doctor fast— the venom can kill in less than two hours.

**STINGER**—*a puncturing organ that can pierce the skin and inject venom*

# STING OF THE SCORPION

Scorpions have stung and killed their prey for more than 400 million years—since long before the age of dinosaurs. These ruthless and efficient hunters often eat their own weight in insects every day, grasping victims with their pincers and then using their stingers to inject venom. Some scorpions also spray their venom in self-defense—it is very painful if it enters the eye.

### Small but deadly
This death-stalker scorpion's venom is dangerous to people, causing pain, fever, breathing difficulties, and even death. When it feels threatened, the 4-in. (10-cm)-long death stalker raises its tail and gets its claws ready to attack.

### Protective poison
A scorpion mother cares for her young. She carries her brood on her back for the first few days of their lives, with her poison-tipped tail curled over them to keep enemies at bay.

*praying mantis stunned by venom*

"Lord! how we suddenly jump, as Scorpio, or the Scorpion, stings us in the rear."

**Stubb**
*second mate on the Pequod in Herman Melville's Moby Dick, 1851*

> More people die from scorpion stings each year in Mexico than in any other country.

## ⊖ HAIRY HUNTER

The rock scorpion lives in southern Africa. It hides in cracks between rocks during the day, coming out to hunt at dusk. Its delicate body hairs can detect vibrations made by any nearby spiders and insects.

Venom is squeezed out of the stinger.

Venom is produced in tiny sacs.

Muscles swing the stinger into position and rock it back and forth.

## Sting in the tail

A yellow fat-tailed scorpion feeds on a praying mantis. Scorpions range in color from yellow and tan to brown and black. Like spiders, they belong to the arachnid family, but they store venom in their muscular tails, not in their fangs. The poison glands and stinger are in the tail's final segment.

http://library.thinkquest.org/27858/general.htm

# DISEASE SPREADERS

Some creatures do not mean to kill, but when they feed on other animals, they pass on germs and diseases. These creatures harbor parasites— tiny organisms that live, feed, and breed inside them. Some mosquitoes, for example, carry a parasite that causes malaria. By spreading it to humans when they bite, these insects kill more people than any other killer creature.

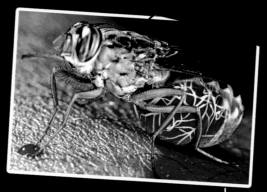

## African killer

Tsetse flies feed on the blood of humans and cattle. They spread a parasite that causes a fatal illness called sleeping sickness in humans.

"A vampire bat . . . needs to drink at least half its body weight every night. Collecting that is not easy."

**David Attenborough (born 1926)**
*British broadcaster and naturalist*

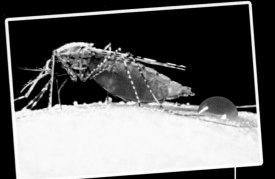

## Mosquito

The female anopheles mosquito spreads malaria. Other species of mosquitoes can spread dengue, yellow fever, and other dangerous diseases.

*A fly's eye, with its thousands of surfaces, is superb at detecting movement.*

*Bacteria on a fly's legs and mouth cause diarrhea and dehydration.*

*A fly spits on its food and then sucks it up through spongy mouthparts.*

## Common as mud

Houseflies feed on animal droppings and rotting material. They carry harmful germs that can contaminate food. The infections they cause kill many children in poorer countries around the world.

## ⊖ MINIATURE KILLERS

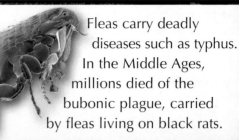

Fleas carry deadly diseases such as typhus. In the Middle Ages, millions died of the bubonic plague, carried by fleas living on black rats.

# Bat attack

Vampire bats drink the blood of sleeping animals. They cut the skin with their sharp front teeth and then lap up the blood. If a bat is carrying the rabies virus, the disease is passed on through the bite. Rabies affects the nervous system and the brain, leading to insanity and death.

*A bat navigates by using echolocation (above). When it nears a victim—such as a sleeping pig—it lands.*

*The bat makes its final approach on all fours. As it feeds, a substance in its saliva keeps the pig's blood flowing.*

# KILLER COLONIES

Which animals form an army and eat every creature in their path? Army ants, which live in the Americas. They march on a million feet across the jungle floor. Cockroaches, scorpions, tarantulas, crickets—all run for their lives. When an army ant finds its prey, it releases a chemical that "calls out" to its comrades. In seconds, hundreds of ants arrive to sting the victim, dismember its body, and carry it back to the nest.

## ANT IN CLOSE-UP

An ant's body has three parts: head, thorax, and abdomen. The head has a mouth, eyes, and antennae. The mouth has two scissorlike jaws called mandibles. Army ants are blind and rely on their antennae to smell, touch, and communicate.

thorax

head

abdomen

"Go to the ant, you lazybones; consider its ways, and be wise."

**Proverbs 6:6, in the Old Testament of the Bible**

### Ant food
Army ants feed mostly on other insects but will kill lizards and snakes. Driver ants, which also form colonies but live in Africa, can smother and kill animals as large as chickens, pigs, and goats if they are cooped or tied up.

> A single colony of army ants can kill and eat up to 100,000 insects in a single day.

*Ant birds perch above the ants, ready to pick off insects fleeing from the colony.*

## Living nests

As army ants move around a forest, they use their own bodies to build temporary nighttime nests called bivouacs. The queen and her eggs are safe in the middle of the mass of ants.

## In a tangle

Ants use their own bodies to build bridges—for example, linking a bivouac to the ground. The individual ants cling together with their clawed feet.

*A large robber fly is ready to snatch any injured insects.*

*Each ant finds its way by detecting chemicals given off by the other ants.*

## Army on the march

A column of army ants snakes across the leaf litter. At the front of the column, the soldiers fan out, covering a 30-ft. (10-m)-wide area. Prey creatures are stung and then hacked into pieces by the ants' jaws. The army makes thousands of kills each day.

# EXTINCT KILLERS

Around 100 million years ago in the swamps of what is now Argentina, there lived a terrifying predator—*Giganotosaurus*. With its huge head, 8-in. (20-cm)-long teeth, clawed hands, and massive, muscular legs, *Giganotosaurus* probably takes the title as the scariest of all the meat-eating dinosaurs. It was even bigger than its North American cousin, *Tyrannosaurus rex*.

The sail-like structure on the back might have been used to regulate body temperature or for display.

## Ferocious theropod

All carnivorous dinosaurs belong to a group that scientists call theropods. *Spinosaurus* was a huge theropod—possibly as long as 59 ft. (18m)—that lived in North Africa 95 million years ago. With its long, crocodilian head, it probably fished rather than hunted on land.

"A single *Giganotosaurus*—even a huge alpha male—is no match for a mature *Argentinosaurus*."

**Henry Gee (born 1962)**
*British paleontologist*

whiplike tail

## Following the herd

*Giganotosaurus* probably lived in small family groups, stalking herds of *Argentinosaurus* and other giant plant eaters as they moved to new feeding grounds. At 115 ft. (35m) long, an adult *Argentinosaurus* was too large to bring down, but small teams of *Giganotosaurus* worked together to pick off younger members of a herd.

> *Giganotosaurus*, whose name means "giant southern lizard," probably measured 46 ft. (14m) from nose to tail.

Deinonychus foot
with huge claw

## Anatomy of a killer

With its long hind legs and light bone structure, *Deinonychus* was a fast sprinter. Each of its feet had one large, curved claw for hooking into prey.

Argentinosaurus *was a sauropod, a long-necked, plant-eating dinosaur.*

6-ft. (1.8-m)-long skull, attached to jawbone lined with 8-in. (20-cm)-long serrated teeth

## ⊖ PACK HUNTERS

*Deinonychus* was an intelligent, speedy, wolf-size predator. It hunted in packs, stalking and ambushing prey. Members of a pack leaped at their victims in a coordinated attack, hanging on with hooklike claws as they bit into the flesh. In this way, *Deinonychus* could hunt prey big enough to provide food for several days.

downy feathers
for warmth

powerful legs
for sprinting

The heavy tail helps counterbalance the enormous head.

www.dinodictionary.com

# GLOSSARY

### abdomen
In animals such as insects and arachnids, the tail end of the body.

### amphibian
A cold-blooded animal that lives on land but breeds in water—for example, a frog.

### antenna (plural: antennae)
In insects, one of a pair of sensory feelers that stick out from the head.

### antivenin
A substance containing proteins that counteract the effects of animal venom.

### bacterium (plural: bacteria)
A simple microorganism. Some bacteria can cause diseases.

### binocular vision
Seeing that involves two eyes working together, allowing the viewer to judge distances. The eyes face forward to give overlapping fields of view.

### blubber
The thick layer of fat beneath a sea mammal's skin that keeps its body warm in the extreme cold.

### camouflage
The use of color or patterns to blend in with the surroundings and escape the notice of predators.

### canine teeth
Also known as fangs or dogteeth, the four pointed teeth at the front of a mammal's mouth on both sides of its incisors, used for gripping meat.

### canopy
The highest part of a rainforest, where the trees spread out their branches.

### carcass
The dead body of an animal.

### carnassial teeth
The large teeth near the back of a carnivore's jaw, used for cutting flesh and bone.

### carnivorous
Describes a flesh-eating animal, especially one from the *Carnivora* order, which includes dogs, cats, and bears.

### carrion
The flesh of a dead animal.

### cold-blooded
Describes an animal that cannot control its own body temperature, which changes according to the animal's surroundings.

### disemboweled
Describes a body when its vital organs have been ripped out.

### echolocation
The way that some animals, such as bats, find their way around and locate prey by making sounds and using the returned echoes to figure out their location.

### extinct
Describes an animal or plant that has died out, never to reappear.

### gland
A group of cells or an organ in the body that produces a particular substance such as poison.

### incisors
A mammal's sharp-edged front teeth.

### ligament
Tough, fibrous tissue that connects muscle to bone.

## mammal
An animal that gives birth to live young, which feed on their mother's milk. Lions and bears are mammals.

## mandibles
In insects, mouthparts used for biting and crushing food.

## marrow
Fatty, protein-rich tissue that fills the hollow center of bones.

## molars
The broad teeth found at the back of a mammal's jaw, used for grinding food.

## nematocyst
A tiny stinging cell that injects venom into prey or an attacker. Jellyfish are armed with nematocysts.

## paleontologist
A scientist who studies the fossils (preserved remains) of extinct animals.

## paralysis
A state in which the body—or part of it—loses the ability to move or feel. Venom can cause paralysis and death.

## polyp
A tiny aquatic creature with a tube-shaped body. Coral reefs build up from the leftover skeletons of dead polyps.

## predator
An animal that hunts and kills other animals.

## prey
An animal that is hunted and killed by other animals.

## rainforest
A thick forest, with very tall trees, that grows in tropical countries where it is hot all year long and rains every day.

## reptile
A cold-blooded animal with scaly skin—for example, a snake. Some reptiles lay eggs and others give birth to live young.

## saliva
Liquid produced in the mouth to make food easier to swallow.

## savanna
An area of grassland and scattered trees found in tropical or subtropical regions.

## scavenger
An animal that feeds on dead animals.

## subtropical
Found in the subtropics—the warm region between the hot tropics and the cooler, temperate parts of the world.

## theropod
A two-legged, carnivorous dinosaur with extremely sharp teeth and claws. All theropods belonged to the saurischian, or lizard-hipped, group of dinosaurs.

## thorax
In animals such as insects, the middle part of the body, found between the head and abdomen.

## toxin
A poisonous substance, especially one formed inside the body.

## tropical
Found in the tropics—the hot parts of the world on both sides of the equator.

## venom
The poisonous fluid that some animals, such as snakes, inject into their prey.

# INDEX

# INVESTIGATE

Encounter killer creatures for yourself in zoos, safari parks, and museum exhibits or find out more on the page or onscreen.

lions at a safari park

## Zoos and safari parks

Visit a zoo or safari park to get up close to a range of predators and learn about breeding programs and other conservation projects to protect animals in the wild.

*Four Corners: Zoos* by Bob Barton (Pearson)

San Diego Zoo, 2920 Zoo Drive, San Diego, CA 92101

www.aza.org

museum exhibit of an animatronic Sydney funnel-web spider

## Museums and exhibits

Natural history museums have displays and expert information about all types of predators, as well as stuffed specimens and dinosaur fossils. Look out for themed exhibits, too.

*The Natural History Museum Book of Predators* by Steve Parker (Carlton)

American Museum of Natural History, Central Park West and 79th Street, New York, NY 10024-5192

www.nhm.ac.uk/nature-online/life/index.html

golden eagle equipped with a documentary camera

illustration from *Biography of a Grizzly* (1900) by Ernest Thompson Seton

## Documentaries and movies

Award-winning documentaries and movies allow you to watch predators displaying natural behavior in their own habitats. Try a close-up IMAX film—if you dare!

*Big Cat Diary: Cheetah* by Jonathan Scott and Angela Scott (HarperCollins)

Mugar Omni Theater, Museum of Science, 1 Science Park, Boston, MA 02114

www.imax.com

## Books and magazines

If you enjoy absorbing facts and looking at amazing photographs, check out some of the many information books and magazines about dangerous animals. Your local librarian might also be able to suggest some exciting narrative accounts of predators.

*Kingfisher Knowledge: Dangerous Creatures* by Angela Wilkes (Kingfisher)

Nature's Best Photography exhibit, Smithsonian National Museum of Natural History, 10th Street and Constitution Avenue NW, Washington, DC 20560

www.nationalgeographic.com/animals